The Best Bourbon

Cookbook

Booze-Infused Sweet & Savory Recipes

Everything tastes better with Bourbon, America's

Native Spirit!

BY

Christina Tosch

Copyright Notes

Table of Contents

Introduction

The Best Bourbon Cookbook featuring 40 sweet and savory recipes will show you how to elevate everyday foods into dinner-party favorites.

From bisques to biscuits, salads to stews, bourbon adds depth and flavor to all sorts of recipes.

Bourbon is not only the perfect tipple for boozy beverages but is also the secret ingredient for appetizers and sides, mains, desserts, and sweet treats.

While you may think that all bourbon is whiskey, the truth is not all whiskey is bourbon! People in the know usually describe it as whiskey's sweet spot.

To earn its name, bourbon has to contain a minimum of 51 percent corn. And the more corn it is made with, the sweeter it tastes. The majority of bourbon distilleries use between 65-75 percent corn.

Read on to find out more fascinating facts about this iconic spirit.

- The law states that bourbon must be barrel-aged for two years
- In Kentucky, barrels of bourbon outnumber people!
- It's official! Bourbon is America's Native Spirit, so say Congress when in 1964, Lyndon B. Johnson awarded bourbon his presidential stamp declaring it The Official Spirit of America
- Although historically used for medicinal purposes, bourbon is an excellent ingredient for cooking and baking, too
- September is National Bourbon Heritage Month

- A staggering 95 percent of the world's bourbon comes from the American state of Kentucky
- As of 2018, there are 68 bourbon distilleries in Kentucky
- Every year on June 14th, the nation raises a glass to this boozy beverage when it celebrates National Bourbon Day

Discover the Best Bourbon Cookbook and get cooking and baking with The Official Spirit of America!

Appetizers & Sides

Apple Arugula Slaw with Orange Bourbon Dressing

Toss a healthy apple and arugula slaw with citrus and boozy dressing, and you will elevate a dull side into an amazing one!

Servings: 4

Total Time: 7mins

Ingredients:

Slaw:

- 1 large-size Granny Smith apple (cored and julienned)
- 2 cups arugula (thinly chopped)
- 1 small-size carrot (peeled and grated)
- 2 green onions (finely sliced)

Dressing:

- ¼ fresh orange juice
- 2 tbsp bourbon
- 2 tsp runny honey
- 2 tbsp mint (chopped)
- 1 tsp Dijon mustard
- 1 tbsp olive oil
- ½ tsp kosher salt
- ¼ tsp black pepper

Directions:

1. In a suitable mixing bowl, toss the apple with the arugula, carrot, and green onions.

2. In a second, large bowl, combine the orange juice with the bourbon, runny honey, mint, mustard, and oil — season with salt and black pepper.

3. Pour the dressing over the slaw mixture and toss to combine.

4. Serve.

Bacon and Bourbon Stuffing

Bacon and bourbon are the perfect combination for a yuletide stuffing and what's more it's way better than any store-bought option.

Servings: 6-8

Total Time: 8hours 50mins

Ingredients:

- 2 French bread loaves (one wheat, one white - cut into small-size cubes)
- 12 ounces cooked bacon
- 1 Granny Smith apples (cored, cut into bite-sized pieces)
- 1 large-size onion (peeled, cut into bite-sized pieces)
- 6 sticks of celery (trimmed, cut into bite-sized pieces)
- 4 garlic cloves (peeled, minced)
- 2 tbsp bourbon
- Salt and black pepper
- 2 cups vegetable broth
- 4 medium-size eggs
- 1 tbsp sage (chopped)
- 1 tbsp thyme (chopped)
- 1 tsp parsley (chopped)

Directions:

1. Arrange the cubes of bread on a large-size baking sheet and allow them to dry out overnight.

2. In a pan, cook the bacon and cut into small bite-size pieces. Set the bacon fat to one side, for later.

3. Cook the apples, onion, celery, and garlic in the bacon fat. Add the bourbon and cook until the ingredients start to soften. Lightly season with salt and black pepper.

4. In a large-size mixing bowl, combine the cooked vegetables with the cooked bacon and dried bread cubes.

5. Stir in the vegetable stock along with the eggs.

6. Stir in the sage, thyme, and parsley.

7. Transfer the mixture to a greased casserole dish and bake in the oven at 375 degrees F for half an hour.

Bourbon and Bacon Deviled Eggs

A popular and classic party appetizer gets a modern makeover with sweet maple syrup and smoky bourbon.

Servings: 24

Total Time: 45mins

Ingredients:

- ¾ tsp Dijon mustard
- 2 tbsp brown sugar
- ½ tsp pure maple syrup
- ⅛ tsp salt
- 2 tsp bourbon
- 4 thickly-sliced strips of bacon

Eggs:

- 12 hard-boiled large-size eggs
- ¾ cup mayonnaise
- 1 tbsp pure maple syrup
- 1 tbsp Dijon mustard
- ¼ tsp pepper
- ¼ tsp ground chipotle pepper
- Fresh chives (minced)

Directions:

1. Preheat the main oven to 350 degrees F.

2. In a bowl, combine ¾ teaspoon of mustard with 2 tbsp brown sugar, and ½ teaspoon of maple syrup, and salt. Stir in the bourbon.

3. Coat the bacon with the brown sugar mixture.

4. Arrange on a baking rack in a 15x10x1" aluminum lined baking pan.

5. Bake in the oven until crisp, for 25-30 minutes. Set aside to completely cool.

6. Slice the eggs in half lengthwise. Remove the yolks and set the whites aside.

7. In a bowl, mash the yolks. Add the mayonnaise, maple syrup, mustard, pepper, and chipotle pepper and stir until silky smooth.

8. Finely chop the bacon and fold half into the egg yolk mixture.

9. Spoon the mixture in the egg whites, garnish with the remaining bacon and minced chives.

10. Cover and transfer to the fridge until you are ready to serve.

Bourbon Chicken Liver Pâté

For a more intense flavor, make this rich appetizer 48 hours in advance.

Servings: 8-10

Total Time: 2hours 35mins

Ingredients:

- ¾ cup unsalted butter (divided)
- 1 cup onion (peeled, finely chopped)
- 1 large-size clove of garlic (peeled, minced)
- ¼ tsp fresh thyme (minced)
- 1 tsp fresh marjoram (minced)
- 1 tsp fresh sage (minced)
- ¾ tsp salt
- ¼ tsp black pepper
- ⅛ tsp allspice
- 1 pound chicken livers (trimmed)
- 2 tbsp bourbon
- Fresh thyme (to garnish)

Directions:

1. Mel ½ a cup of butter over medium-low heat in a large frying pan or skillet.

2. Cook the onion along with the garlic, while stirring for 5 minutes, until softened.

3. Add the thyme, marjoram, sage, salt, pepper, and allspice followed by the chicken livers and cook while stirring for approximately 8 minutes, or until the liver is cooked on the outside but pink when cut open.

4. Stir in the bourbon and remove the pan from the heat.

5. Puree the mixture in a food blender/processor until silky smooth.

6. Transfer the pate to a terrine and smooth over the top.

7. Melt the remaining butter in a small heavy pan over low heat.

8. Remove the pan from the stovetop and allow the butter to stand for a few minutes.

9. Garnish with fresh thyme.

10. Skim any froth from the butter and spoon sufficiently clarified butter over the surface of the pate to cover its entire surface. Leave the milky solids in the bottom of the pan.

11. Chill the pate in the fridge until the butter is firm, for half an hour. Cover with kitchen wrap and chill in the refrigerator for an additional 2 hours.

Cook's Note: You can store pate in the fridge for up to 14 days. However, once the surface of the pate is broken and the butter seal no longer intact, cover with a piece of kitchen wrap.

Bourbon-Glazed Chicken Wings with Sweet Chili Sauce

A sports bar favorite, these crisp chicken wings are not only glazed in bourbon but also served with a sweet chili bourbon sauce. What's more, you don't have to leave the comfort of your home to enjoy them!

Servings: 30

Total Time: 4hours

Ingredients:

- 30 good-quality chicken wings
- 3 ounces premium bourbon
- 2 tbsp kosher salt
- 2 tbsp dark brown sugar
- 2 tbsp Tabasco hot sauce
- 2 cloves of garlic (peeled, crushed)
- Nonstick cooking spray

Chili Sauce:

- 3 ounces premium bourbon
- 1 cup store-bought sweet chili sauce
- 1 tbsp Sriracha chili sauce

Directions:

1. For the wings: In a large container, combine the wings with the bourbon, salt, dark brown sugar, Tabasco hot sauce, and the garlic. Mix thoroughly and transfer to the fridge for ½-3 hours.

2. Preheat the main oven to 425 degrees F. Using a parchment paper line a baking sheet. Spray the paper with nonstick spray.

3. Arrange the wings in a single layer and not touch one another on the baking sheet.

4. Bake the wings in the oven for 20-25 minutes, or until cooked through. The internal temperature of the wings should register 165 degrees F when using a meat thermometer.

5. For the sauce: Combine the bourbon with the sweet chili sauce and Sriracha and mix until entirely incorporated.

6. Remove the wings from the oven and brush all over with the chili sauce. Return the wings to the oven for 3-5 minutes before serving.

7. Pour the remaining sauce over the wings and toss until coated evenly. Serve!

Cheesy Sausage Bites with Bourbon Mustard Dipping Sauce

This classic appetizer from the Deep South is a must-have. Crisp and cheese sausage bites to serve with a creamy sweet bourbon dipping sauce is definitely sure to be one of your favorite at your next party.

Servings: 4-6

Total Time: 1hour

Ingredients:

- 2 sleeves saltine crackers (crushed)
- 2 medium-size eggs
- ½ cup buttermilk
- 2 pounds good-quality country sausage
- 1½ cups Cheddar cheese (freshly shredded)

Dipping Sauce:

- 1 cup mayonnaise
- ⅓cup yellow mustard
- 2 tbsp runny honey
- 3 ounces premium bourbon

Directions:

1. Preheat the main oven to 450 degrees F.

2. In a mixing bowl, combine the crackers with the egg and buttermilk.

3. Next, add the sausage and Cheddar cheese. Mix to combine while making sure not to overwork.

4. Cover the bowl and set aside in the fridge for half an hour, to cool.

5. Using washed hands, form the mixture into balls, and arrange on greased cookie sheets.

6. Bake in the oven for 12 minutes. Check the cooking process and bake for an additional 5-6 minutes, or until cooked through. The bites should be gently browned with a crunchy exterior.

7. For the dipping sauce: In a bowl, combine the mayonnaise with the mustard, honey, and bourbon. Stir well to combine.

8. Serve the bites with a side of dipping sauce and enjoy.

Cook's Note: Serve any leftovers in the fridge for up to 7 days

Coconut-Bourbon Sweet Potatoes

Create the perfect fall or winter dish to serve alongside any holiday feast. This recipe is sure to become your go-to side.

Servings: 12-14

Total Time: 1hour

Ingredients:

- 8 cups sweet potato mash
- ¾ cup half & half cream
- ½ cup packed brown sugar
- ½ cup bourbon
- 2 large eggs
- ¼ cup honey
- 3 tsp vanilla essence
- 1¼ tsp ground cinnamon
- ¼ tsp salt
- 1 tbsp molasses
- ½ tsp ground cardamom
- 1 cup sweetened shredded coconut
- ¾ cup golden raisins
- 1½ cups mini marshmallows

Topping:

- ½ cup all-purpose flour
- ½ cup packed brown sugar
- 1 tsp ground cinnamon
- ⅓ cup butter (melted)
- 1 cup pecans (chopped)

Directions:

1. In a suitable bowl, combine the sweet potato mash with the half and half, brown sugar, bourbon, eggs, honey, vanilla essence, ground cinnamon, and salt.

2. Next, add the molasses and cardamom.

3. Stir in the coconut and golden raisins.

4. Move the mixture to a 13x9" casserole dish.

5. Sprinkle mini mallows evenly over the top.

6. For the topping: In a small-size bowl, combine the flour with the brown sugar and cinnamon. Add the butter, mixing until a crumbly consistency.

7. Mix the chopped pecans and sprinkle the mixture over the mini mallows.

8. Let bake in the oven at 350 degrees F until heated through and golden. This will take 35-40 minutes.

9. Serve.

Shrimp Bisque with Bourbon

Smooth, creamy, and perfectly seasoned, this rich soup featuring juicy shrimp and smoky bourbon is a sophisticated appetizer.

Servings: 8

Total Time: 2hours

Ingredients:

- 2 pounds large shrimp
- 2 tbsp olive oil (divid3ed)
- 2 tsp salt (divided)
- ½ tsp freshly ground black pepper (divided)
- ¼ cup + 3 tbsp bourbon (divided)
- 3 tbsp unsalted butter (divided)
- ¾ cup celery
- ¾ cup fennel
- 1 large-size onion (peeled, thinly sliced)
- 3 garlic cloves (peeled, chopped)
- 3 tbsp tomato paste
- 2 tbsp all-purpose flour
- ½ cup white wine
- 5 cups water
- ½ cup low-salt chicken broth
- ½ cup basmati rice
- ½ tsp dried rosemary
- ½ tsp dried thyme
- 8 tbsp heavy cream

Directions:

1. First, cook the shrimp. Peel, de-vein, and while setting 16 whole shrimp aside, roughly chop the rest. Reserve the shells.

2. At high heat, heat 1 tablespoon of oil in a 12" Dutch oven.

3. Season the shrimp with ¼ teaspoon of salt and a ¼ teaspoon of pepper.

4. Cook the chopped shrimp until they are just opaque.

5. Add the remaining olive oil along with the shrimp shells (set aside in Step 1) to the pan and while occasionally stirring, cooking until the shells begin to brown.

6. Pour in ¼ cup of bourbon, and while continually stirring, cook the mixture is reduced by approximately half.

7. Transfer the shrimp shells along with the liquid to a mixing bowl and put it to one side.

8. For the soup: Over moderate heat, melt 1 tablespoon of butter in the pan.

9. Add the celery along with the fennel and cook for 10 minutes.

10. Next, add the onions, garlic, remaining salt, and remaining pepper and cook until the onions are softened.

11. Fill the tomato paste and cook until it starts to coat the bottom of the pan.

12. Fill 1 tablespoon of butter to the pan and melt.

13. While continually stirring, add the flour and cook until incorporated.

14. Pour in the wine, water, and chicken broth, and add the rice, rosemary, thyme and shrimp shells. Bring to simmer.

15. Cook until the basmati rice is bite-tender, for 30-35 minutes.

16. Process the soup and shrimp shells through a food mill. Remove and discard the solids and return the mixture to pan over low heat.

17. Add the chopped shrimp, heavy cream and remaining bourbon, and cook until heated through.

18. Over high heat, in a small frying pan, melt the remaining butter.

19. Sauté the 16 whole shrimp set aside in Step 1 for 4 minutes, or until cooked through.

20. Serve the soup into individual bowls, garnish with the shrimp and enjoy.

Slow Cooker Bourbon Meatballs

These meatballs in a bourbon sauce are party perfect. Serve as an appetizer and enjoy.

Servings: 4-6

Total Time: 2hours 5mins

Ingredients:

- ½ cup ketchup
- ½ cup brown sugar
- ¼ cup bourbon
- 1 tsp freshly squeezed lemon juice
- 1 tsp Worcestershire sauce
- 1 pound frozen meatballs

Directions:

1. In a suitable bowl, combine the ketchup with the brown sugar, bourbon, fresh lemon juice, and Worcestershire sauce. Mix to combine.

2. Add the frozen meatballs to your slow cooker.

3. Pour the sauce over the meatballs, stir well to cover entirely.

4. In a slow cooker, cook on high for 60 minutes, then on low for 60 minutes.

5. Serve and enjoy.

Winter Salad with Maple Bourbon Dressing

Jazz up a winter salad featuring sweet potatoes, mixed greens, and crunchy nuts with a boozy bourbon dressing.

Servings: 4

Total Time: 1hour 5mins

Ingredients:

- 1 large-size sweet potato (peeled, diced into ½" cubes)
- 6 chestnuts (rinsed and dried)
- 2 tbsp extra-virgin olive oil
- ½ tsp salt
- 1 (5 ounce) package baby spinach and kale mix
- 1 small-size shallot (halved and thinly shaved)
- ¼ cup pomegranate arils

Bourbon Dressing:

- ¼ cup pure maple syrup
- 3 tbsp bourbon
- ¼ cup apple cider vinegar
- 1 tsp Dijon mustard
- ½ cup extra-virgin olive oil

Directions:

1. Preheat the main oven to 425 degrees F.

2. First, roast the sweet potato along with the chestnuts. Add the sweet potato to a bowl and toss with the oil and salt.

3. Arrange the sweet potato, in a single and even layer on a baking sheet.

4. Place the baking sheet in the oven for 40 minutes, or until roasted.

5. With a paring knife, make ⅛" incisions in the chestnut skins and cut across the nut. This will prevent the nuts from exploding while cooking and make them easier to peel.

6. Once the sweet potatoes have reached the halfway cooking mark, add the chestnuts to the baking sheet, and return to the oven for an additional 20 minutes.

7. Remove the baking sheet from the oven and set aside to cool for 5 minutes. Peel the chestnuts.

8. For the salad: In a large-size salad bowl, add the spinach and kale mix.

9. Sprinkle the shaved shallots over the green and top with the roasted sweet potatoes.

10. Scatter the pomegranate arils over the top and using clean hands, crumble small pieces of the nuts over the top.

11. For the Dressing: In a pan, while whisking, combine the maple syrup with the bourbon, apple cider vinegar, mustard, and olive oil. On low heat, simmer for 5 minutes.

12. Drizzle the salad with the homemade warm maple bourbon dressing and gently toss.

13. Serve or allow to cool for 10-15 minutes, depending on your preference.

Mains

Beef and Bourbon Stew

This stew is a real winter warmer. It's hearty, satisfying, and served with slices of French baguette, it makes a mouthwatering meal to share with friends or family.

Servings: 4-6

Total Time: 4hours 15mins

Ingredients:

- ½ cup all-purpose flour
- Salt and black pepper (to season)
- 2 pounds 2 ounces beef steak (chopped)
- ¼ cup bourbon
- 1 garlic clove (peeled and minced)
- 1 onion (peeled and sliced)
- 1 cup mushrooms (sliced)
- 3 carrots (sliced into thick circles)
- Italian seasoning (to taste)
- 1-quart beef stock
- 1 (15 ounce) can diced tomatoes
- 1 (15 ounce) can tomato soup

Directions:

1. Sprinkle the flour onto the bottom of the slow cooker. Season the flour with salt and pepper.

2. Add the beef and toss to coat in the seasoned flour evenly.

3. Pour in the bourbon and slightly stir.

4. Add the garlic, onion, mushrooms, carrots, Italian seasoning (to taste), and the beef stock.

5. Stir in the diced tomatoes and tomato soup.

6. Cook on low for 3-4 hours until the meat is cooked through and the veggies bite-tender.

7. Serve and enjoy.

Bourbon Chicken

This dish got its name from the famous Bourbon Street in N'Awlins. It combines the Asian flavor of soy sauce with southern bourbon.

Servings: 6

Total Time: 55mins

Ingredients:

- 3 pounds of chicken thighs' boneless, skinless (cut into 1" bite-sized pieces)
- 4 tbsp olive oil
- 1 cup water
- 1 cup packed brown sugar
- ¾ cup chicken broth
- ⅔ cup low-sodium soy sauce
- ¼ cup ketchup
- ¼ cup bourbon
- 2 tbsp apple cider vinegar
- 5 cloves garlic (peeled and minced)
- 1 small-size onion (peeled and minced)
- ¾ tsp crushed red pepper flakes
- 1½ tbsp freshly grated ginger
- ¼ cup fresh apple juice
- 2 tbsp cornstarch

Directions:

1. In a strong 12" Dutch oven, heat the oil.

2. Place the chicken and cook until lightly golden all over, for approximately 10 minutes.

3. Using a slotted spoon, remove the chicken from the Dutch oven and tent with aluminum foil to keep the chicken warm. It will not be entirely cooked through at this stage.

4. In the now-empty Dutch oven, add the water along with the sugar, broth, soy sauce, ketchup, bourbon, vinegar, garlic, onion, red pepper flakes, and ginger.

5. Bring the mixture to boil, and with a wooden spoon, scrape up any browned bits from the bottom.

6. Transfer the chicken to the Dutch oven along with the sauce and any of the chicken juices again.

7. Slightly turn the heat down to moderately low and allow to simmer for 20 minutes, until the chicken is totally cooked through and the sauce has begun to thicken.

8. In a bowl, whisk the apple juice with the corn starch. Stir into the Dutch oven with a wooden spoon and increase the heat to moderate-high and bring to boil for 60 seconds, while continually stirring, to thicken.

9. Serve while hot and enjoy with a serving of rice and corn.

Bourbon-Spiked Mac n Cheese

A classic all-American meal gets a boozy bourbon makeover. This sensational recipe is full of cheesy goodness and taste.

Servings: 4

Total Time: 55mins

Ingredients:

- Nonstick cooking spray
- ½ cup + 1 tbsp bourbon (divided)
- 2 tbsp brown sugar
- 1 tsp cayenne pepper
- 10 rashers of bacon
- 1 pound elbow macaroni
- 3 tbsp unsalted butter
- ⅓ cup all-purpose flour
- 2 cups whole milk (divided)
- 3 cups mature Cheddar cheese
- 4 slices Provolone cheese
- ½ tsp paprika
- Salt and black pepper

Directions:

1. Preheat the main oven to 400 degrees. Using aluminum foil sprayed with nonstick cooking spray line a baking sheet.

2. In a pan, over high heat bring ½ a cup of bourbon to boil.

3. Slightly reduce the heat to moderate and simmer until the alcohol reduces to approximately 2 tablespoons.

4. Remove the pan from the heat.

5. On a dessert plate, combine the brown sugar with the cayenne pepper.

6. One at a time, dip the slices of bacon first in the bourbon, and second in the brown sugar mixture evenly coating on both sides.

7. Arrange the slices of bacon on the baking sheet.

8. Bake in the oven and cook for 7 minutes before flipping over and baking for 5 minutes, while taking care the bacon doesn't burn.

9. Move the bacon from the baking sheet and place it on a serving plate coated with nonstick cooking spray.

10. Chop the bacon when sufficiently cool and put it to one side.

11. Bring a deep pan of water to boil.

12. Add the pasta to the boiling water and cook until al dente. Drain the pasta and set it to one side.

13. Meanwhile, while the pasta cooks, over moderate-high heat, in a deep-sided pan, melt the butter.

14. Add the flour and whisk to combine entirely.

15. Stir in the remaining tablespoonful of bourbon and whisk to combine.

16. Fill in 1 cup of milk and whisk to incorporate.

17. Add the remaining milk and frequently whisk until the sauce begins to bubble and thicken.

18. Whisk in the Cheddar and provolone cheeses until melted and combined to create a smooth sauce.

19. Mix the paprika and season with salt and black pepper.

20. Pour the sauce over the drained pasta, mix to combine, and stir in the chopped bacon.

21. Serve and enjoy.

Brown Sugar Steak with Bourbon

If you like red meat, then you will love this recipe. A brown sugar, bourbon, and red pepper flake marinade add taste and tenderness to a juicy, medium-rare steak.

Servings: 4

Total Time: 2hours 30mins

Ingredients:

- 1½ pounds flank steak
- ¼ cup brown sugar
- ½ tsp red pepper flakes
- ¼ cup bourbon
- Kosher salt

Directions:

1. In a bowl, layer the steak with the sugar, red pepper flakes, and bourbon.

2. Rub the sugar mixture into the steak.

3. Add the steak to a 1-gallon ziplock bag. Add the remaining sugar mixture and seal the bag. Allow it to rest in the refrigerator for ½-3 hours.

4. Heat your grill or broiler and arrange the steak on a baking sheet.

5. Liberally season the steak all over with kosher salt.

6. Put the steak under the broiler, approximately 4-6" away from the flame. For medium-rare, broil for 3 minutes on each side.

7. Take the steak out from under the broiler, and place on a chopping board. Set aside resting for 5-10 minutes before cutting into ¼" slices.

Cherry and Bourbon Glazed Meatloaf

A meaty treat with a fruity twist, this homemade meatloaf is a classic family favorite.

Servings: 6-8

Total Time: 40mins

Ingredients:

Bourbon Glaze:

- 1 cup smooth cherry jam
- ¼ cup dark brown sugar
- 1 tbsp hot chili sauce
- ½ cup bourbon
- ½ cup of your favorite BBQ sauce
- ¼ cup water

Meatloaf:

- 1 pound ground pork
- 1 pound ground beef
- 1 egg (beaten)
- ½ cup fresh breadcrumbs
- ½ yellow onion (peeled and minced)
- 1 tsp salt
- Freshly cracked black pepper

Directions:

1. Preheat the oven to 350 degrees F,

2. For the sauce: Add the cherry jam to the dark brown sugar, hot chili sauce, bourbon, BBQ sauce, and water and stir well to incorporate. Bring the glaze to boil and reduce the heat to a simmer or gentle boil and uncovered cook until thickened, for 10 minutes.

3. To make the meatloaf: Add the pork and beef to a large-size mixing bowl, using the back of your wooden spoon to separate the meat up into small pieces.

4. Add the beaten egg along with the breadcrumbs, onion, salt, and pepper to the mixing bowl, and using clean fingers combine well.

5. Form the meat mixture into an evenly shaped loaf.

6. Place the loaf directly on a baking sheet lined with foil.

7. Spread a layer of bourbon glaze over the loaf and allow it to rest for 3 minutes before slicing.

8. Spread on another coat of glaze and serve.

Chipotle Bourbon Pumpkin Chili

This meat-free bourbon-infused pumpkin chili will pleasantly surprise all your family and friends.

Servings: 6

Total Time: 1hour

Ingredients:

- 1 tbsp grapeseed oil
- 1 medium-size onion (peeled and minced)
- 3 garlic cloves (peeled and minced)
- 1 red pepper (diced)
- 2 tsp chili powder
- 1 tsp cumin
- 1 tsp sea salt
- ½ cup bourbon
- 14 ounces canned pumpkin (not puree)
- 1 (28 ounce) can crushed tomatoes
- 1 (18½ ounce) can navy beans
- 1 (18½ ounce) can of kidney beans
- 1 tbsp chipotle peppers pureed with adobo sauce
- 1 small-size butternut squash (cut into 1" cubes)
- 2 cups frozen corn
- White Cheddar cheese (grated, to serve)
- Green onions (chopped, to serve)

Directions:

1. Over medium-high heat, in a deep pot, warm the oil.

2. Add the onion to the pot and sauté for 7-8 minutes, until soft and browned.

3. Next, add the garlic along with the red pepper and continue cooking for 5 minutes, until the red pepper softens. Add the chili powder, cumin, and sea salt and allow it to cook for an additional 60 seconds.

4. Pour in the bourbon and bring to boil

5. Add the canned pumpkin followed by the tomatoes, navy beans, kidney beans, pureed chipotle peppers, butternut squash, and 2 cups of water. Stir well to combine.

6. Cover with a suitable lid and bring to boil before reducing the heat and allowing the chili to stew for half an hour, or until the butternut squash is fork-tender.

7. Next, add the frozen corn and allow it to cook for 5 minutes — season with sea salt.

8. Scatter the Cheddar and green onions over the chili and serve.

Orange, Bourbon, and Molasses Glazed Roasted Duck

The perfect holiday roast to suit any special occasion or seasonal holiday.

Servings: 8-10

Total Time: 11hours 50mins

Ingredients:

- 2 (6 pound) whole ducks (remove and discard giblets)
- 2 tsp kosher salt
- ½ tsp freshly ground black pepper
- 1 cup orange marmalade
- ¼ cup bourbon
- 3 tbsp molasses
- 1 tbsp freshly squeezed lemon juice
- ¼ tsp ground ginger
- ¼ tsp dried crushed red pepper

Directions:

1. Rinse the ducks and pat dry using kitchen paper towels. Remove the excess fat and skin.

2. Tie the duck's legs together using kitchen string and chill in the fridge, uncovered for 10-24 hours.

3. Preheat the main oven to 450 degrees F.

4. Allow the ducks to stand for 15 minutes at room temperature.

5. Using a metal fork, prick the legs, thighs, and breasts.

6. Brush salt and black pepper all over the ducks.

7. Place the ducks, breast side facing upwards, on a wire baking rack, in an aluminum foil-lined jelly-roll tin and bake in the oven for 45 minutes.

8. In the meantime, in a pan, stir the orange marmalade with the bourbon, molasses, lemon juice, ginger, and crushed red pepper. Over high heat, bring to boil.

9. Turn the heat down to moderate and while frequently stirring cook for 10-15 minutes, until the mixture reduces to approximately 1 cup.

10. Take the ducks out of the oven and spoon the fat from the pan.

11. Brush the duck all over with the orange marmalade glaze.

12. Turn oven's temperature down to 350 degrees F and bake for 20-25 minutes, until the meat registers 180 degrees F on a meat thermometer.

13. Let rest the duck for 15 minutes before serving.

Pan-Seared Cod with Bourbon Sauce

A honey-bourbon sauce to serve over flaky pan-fried cod is perfect for sharing with your significant fish-loving other.

Servings: 2

Total Time: 15mins

Ingredients:

- 2 (4 ounce) cod fillets
- ¼ cup balsamic vinegar
- ¼ cup bourbon
- ¼ cup honey
- 1 tbsp butter
- ½ tbsp olive oil
- 1 tsp salt

Directions:

1. Using kitchen paper towels, pat the fish dry, and then pat it once again. Set aside to rest until it comes to room temperature.

2. In the meantime, pour the balsamic vinegar and bourbon, combine and put it to one side.

3. Pour the honey into a small pot and heat for 1-2 minutes over moderate heat until it begins to bubble. Using a wooden spoon, stir until the honey darkens in color and becomes an amber color or 3 minutes. At this point, the honey will be very hot, so take care.

4. Standing well back from the pot to avoid splashbacks, pour the balsamic mixture into the honey. Cook while stirring for an additional 1-2 minutes. Remove from the heat and put to one side.

5. In a pan, over moderately high heat, heat the butter with the oil.

6. Season the cod with salt on both sides.

7. Place the cod in the hot pan and leave it to cook without disturbing for 4 minutes exactly. Should the butter begin to smoke, reduce the heat slightly. Using a metal spatula and once the fish isn't sticking to the pan, flip it over.

8. Cook the fish for an additional 4 minutes before placing on dinner plates.

9. Serve immediately along with the bourbon sauce.

Slow Cooker Bourbon Baked Beans

Catering for a hungry crowd? Then this Over-21 version of baked beans will satisfy even the most challenging taste buds. Serve with chunks of crusty bread.

Servings: 15-20

Total Time: 4hours 15mins

Ingredients:

- 6 slices of bacon
- 1 cup onion (peeled, chopped)
- 3 (14½ ounce) cans pork and beans (undrained)
- 1 (14½ ounce) can Navy beans (drained, rinsed)
- 1 (14½ ounce) can Northern beans (drained, rinsed)
- ¾ cup ketchup
- ¼ cup molasses
- ¼ cup brown sugar
- 2 tbsp yellow mustard
- ¼ cup bourbon
- 1 tbsp Worcestershire sauce
- ½ tsp black pepper
- ½ tsp salt
- ¼ tsp garlic powder
- ¼ tsp cayenne pepper

Directions:

1. In a skillet, cook the bacon. Transfer the cooked bacon to a paper towel-lined plate. Set 1 tablespoon of bacon side aside and discard the rest.

2. Fry the onion in the bacon fat for between 3-4 minutes.

3. Add the onions, pork and beans, Navy beans, Northern beans, ketchup, molasses, brown sugar, yellow mustard, bourbon, Worcestershire sauce, black pepper, salt, garlic powder and cayenne to a crockpot of 6-quart capacity. Stir to combine, cover with the lid, and on low cook for 4 hours.

4. Remove the lid, increase the heat to high, and cook for an additional 20 minutes to thicken.

5. Stir in the cooked bacon and serve.

Spiced Pork Medallions with Bourbon

A restaurant-worthy main in just 20 minutes! Now that's what we call a real dinner-party lifesaver.

Servings: 4

Total Time: 20mins

Ingredients:

- ½ cup bourbon
- 3 tbsp white vinegar
- ¼ cup packed dark brown sugar
- 3 tbsp reduced-sodium soy sauce
- 2 cloves of garlic (peeled and minced)
- ½ tsp pepper
- ½ tsp chili powder
- ¼ tsp ground cinnamon
- ⅛ tsp salt
- ⅛ tsp ground allspice
- 1 (1 pound) pork tenderloin (cut into 12 slices)
- Nonstick cooking spray

Directions:

1. In a pan, combine the bourbon with the white vinegar, brown sugar, pepper, soy sauce, and garlic. Bring the mixture to boil and cook while occasionally stirring until the liquid reduced to ½ cup.

2. In the meantime, combine the chili powder with the cinnamon, salt, and allspice. Rub the mixture over the slices of pork.

3. Spritz a large frying pan with nonstick cooking spray.

4. Cook the pork over moderate heat for 2-4 minutes, on each side, until tender and cooked through. The inside temperature of the meat should enroll 145 degrees F on a thermometer.

5. Serve with the sauce.

Desserts & Sweet Treats

Boozy Caramel Popcorn

Give this kiddie favorite a grown-up makeover by adding bourbon to the mix.

Servings: 20

Total Time: 1hour 1mins

Ingredients:

- 20 cups popped popcorn
- ⅓ cup bourbon
- 1 cup unsalted butter (cubed)
- 2 cups packed light brown sugar
- ½ cup light corn syrup
- ¼ tsp cream of tartar
- ¼ tsp salt
- ½ tsp bicarbonate of soda

Directions:

1. Preheat the main oven to 250 degrees F.

2. Add the popcorn to a large size bowl.

3. In a pan, bring the bourbon to boil.

4. Turn the heat down and simmer, while uncovered, for a couple of minutes.

5. Add the butter, and on low cook until melted.

6. Stir in the brown sugar along with the corn syrup, cream of tartar, and salt.

7. Bring to boil, and cook for an additional 5 minutes, while occasionally stirring.

8. Move the pan out from the heat and stir in the bicarbonate of soda. Working quickly, pour over popcorn, and thoroughly mix.

9. Transfer to 2 greased (15x10x1") baking pans and bake in the oven for 60 minutes, until dry, stirring every 15 minutes or so.

10. Remove the popcorn from the pans and place on wax paper to cool.

Bourbon Ice Cream

This no-churn ice cream makes a tempting treat for bourbon-lovers. Why not try some with your Christmas pudding?

Servings: 8-10

Total Time: 20mins

Ingredients:

- 2 cups heavy whipping cream
- 1 (14 ounce) can sweetened condensed milk
- 1½-2 tbsp vanilla bean paste
- 3 tbsp bourbon

Directions:

1. In a suitable mixing bowl, beat the heavy whipping cream on moderate-high speed until stiff peaks form, for approximately 4 minutes.

2. In a second, smaller-size bowl, add the condensed milk with the vanilla bean paste, and bourbon and whisk well to incorporate.

3. Fill the condensed milk into the whipped cream and fold together until thoroughly mixed.

4. Transfer the mixture to a 9x5" loaf pan and with a blunt knife, smooth the surface.

5. Lid with aluminum foil and place in the freezer overnight.

Brownie Bourbon Bites

Pop-in-the-mouth perfections, these brownie bites are the ideal after-dinner sweet treat to enjoy with liqueurs or coffee.

Servings: 24

Total Time: 1hour 40mins

Ingredients:

- ½ cup butter (softened)
- ½ cup packed brown sugar
- ¼ cup bourbon
- 1 cup all-purpose flour
- 3 tbsp baking cocoa
- ½ cup miniature semi-sweet chocolate chips
- 1 cup pecans (roughly chopped)

Directions:

1. In a suitable bowl, cream the butter with the sugar until fluffy and light.

2. Beat in the bourbon.

3. Combine the flour with the baking cocoa, and a little at a time add it to the butter-sugar mixture, beating well until silky smooth.

4. Stir in the semi-sweet chocolate chips.

5. lid the bowl and place in the fridge for 1-2 hours.

6. Using clean hands, shape the mixture into 1" ball-shapes.

7. Roll the balls in the pecans and arrange 2" apart on ungreased baking sheets.

8. Bake in the oven at 350 degrees F for 8-10 minutes, until set.

9. Allow to cool for 5 minutes.

10. Take out from the pans and set aside to cool on wire baking racks.

11. Store in a re-sealable airtight container.

Bundt Cake with Toffee Bourbon Sauce

If you are planning a celebration, then this spicy Bundt cake served with a toffee bourbon sauce is ideal.

Servings: 8

Total Time: 2hours 40mins

Ingredients:

- Nonstick cooking spray
- 1 tsp baking powder
- 2¼ cups flour
- 1 tsp bicarbonate of soda
- ½ tsp salt
- ½ tsp cloves
- 1 tsp cinnamon
- ½ tsp pepper
- ¼ tsp cardamom
- 8 tbsp butter
- ½ cup brown sugar
- 1 cup sugar
- 2 medium-size eggs
- 1 tsp vanilla essence
- Zest of 1 orange
- 1¼ cups buttermilk

Toffee Sauce:

- ½ cup butter
- 1 cup brown sugar
- ½ cup light corn syrup
- 1 (14 ounce) can sweetened condensed milk
- 3 tbsp premium bourbon
- 1 tsp pure vanilla bean extract
- Pinch of salt

Directions:

1. Preheat main oven to 350 degrees F. Spray the inside of a Bundt pan with nonstick cooking spray.

2. In a bowl, sift in the baking powder, flour, bicarbonate of soda, salt, cloves, cinnamon, pepper, and cardamom.

3. To the suitable bowl of a stand mixer, add the butter with the sugar and brown sugar. Beat and cream for 5 minutes, until fluffy.

4. On medium speed, one at a time, add the eggs and mix until entirely combined. Add the vanilla essence and orange zest.

5. Continue mixing, and alternately add the sifted flour-cardamom mixture along with the buttermilk to the cake batter. Beat for 60 seconds until smooth.

6. Fill the cake batter into the prepared Bundt pan and bake in the preheated oven for 40-50 minutes, until a cocktail stick pulls out clean.

7. Remove the pan from the oven and set aside to cool for 15 minutes.

8. To release the cake while still warm, invert the pan onto a cake platter.

9. Allow the cake to completely cool before adding the sauce.

10. For the toffee sauce: Over moderate heat, in a pan, melt the butter.

11. As soon as the butter is halfway melted, stir in the brown sugar, corn syrup, condensed milk, and bourbon.

12. Cook while stirring until the sauce is no longer grainy, is light caramel in color and thickened.

13. Take out of the heat and stir in the vanilla bean extract.

14. Pour the sauce over the now cooled Bundt cake and enjoy.

Chocolate Bourbon Pecan Tart

Chocolate tart crossed with pecan pie is a culinary match made in dessert heaven. So, enjoy!

Servings: 12

Total Time:

Ingredients:

- 1 (9") single-crust pie
- ½ cup semi-sweet chocolate chips
- 2 large-size eggs (room temperature)
- ¾ cup dark corn syrup
- ½ cup sugar
- ¼ cup butter (melted)
- 2 tbsp bourbon
- ¼ tsp salt
- 1 cup pecan halves (toasted)
- ¼ cup hot caramel ice cream topping

Directions:

1. Preheat the main oven to 375 degrees.

2. On a delicately floured worktop, roll the batter out into a 12" circle.

3. Crush the dough onto the bottom and up the sides of an ungreased 11" springform tart pan. Sprinkle with chocolate chips.

4. In a fitting bowl, beat the eggs with the corn syrup, sugar, butter, bourbon, and salt.

5. Fold in the pecans and pour over the chocolate chips.

6. Bake in the oven until the middle is set and crust is golden, for approximately 30-35 minutes.

7. Set aside to cool on wire baking rack before cutting into slices.

8. Serve with the caramel topping.

Christmas Pudding

Banish the brandy and relegate the rum, bourbon is the star of the show for this rich and fruity Christmas pudding.

Servings: 20

Total Time 7hours

Ingredients:

- 1 (13 ounce) packet raisins (chopped)
- ¾ cup currants
- 1 (13 ounce) packet sultanas
- ¾ cup prunes (chopped)
- 1 cup water
- ½ cup caster sugar
- ½ cup firmly packed dark brown sugar
- 4⅓ ounces butter (chopped)
- 1 tsp bicarbonate of soda
- 2 eggs (lightly whisked)
- 1 cup plain flour
- 1 cup self-rising flour
- 1 tsp mixed spice
- ½ tsp ground cinnamon
- 2 tbsp bourbon
- Custard or cream (to serve, optional)

Directions:

1. Grease an 8-cup capacity pudding basin and using baking paper line the basin.

2. In a pan, over low heat, mingle the raisins with the currants, sultanas, prunes, water, caster sugar, brown sugar, and butter. Cook for 4-5 minutes until the butter melts and sugar entirely dissolves.

3. Turn the heat to high and bring to boil before reducing to moderate-low heat and simmer for 10 minutes, or until the dried fruit softens and the mixture thickens.

4. Remove the pan from the heat and add the bicarb, stirring to incorporate.

5. Put to one side to entirely cool.

6. Add the eggs, plain flour, self-rising flour, mixed spice, cinnamon, and bourbon and stir with a wooden spoon until incorporated.

7. Transfer the mixture to the pudding basin and cover it with a secure lid.

8. Place the basin in a large pot and pour in sufficient boiling water to fill halfway up the sides of the pudding basin.

9. Cover with a tight-fitting lid and put on the stovetop over moderate-low heat and slowly bring to slow boil.

10. Cook the pudding for approximately 5 hours, until sufficiently cooked through. You may need to add more boiling water.

11. Take out of the pot from the heat and set to one side to stand for 10 minutes before place on a plate.

12. Serve the Christmas pudding with custard or cream.

Kentucky Bourbon Balls

Indulge your sweet tooth with this best-ever southern candy.

Servings: 30

Total Time: 9hours 35mins

Ingredients:

- 1 cup pecans (finely chopped)
- 5 tbsp bourbon
- ½ cup butter (softened)
- 4 cups confectioner's sugar
- 3 cups semi-sweet chocolate chips
- 3 tbsp shortening
- 30 pecan halves

Directions:

1. In a bowl, combine the pecans with the bourbon. Cover and set aside at room temperature overnight.

2. Using your electric mixer, whip the butter and gradually add the confectioner's sugar.

3. Once the mixture is entirely combined, add the pecan-bourbon mixture and combine. You may need to add more sugar if the mixture's consistency is too soft.

4. Using a teaspoonful of the mixture, form into 30 (1") balls.

5. Organize the balls in a single layer on a parchment-lined baking sheet, and place in the fridge for 60 minutes, until firm.

6. Over low heat, in a suitable heavy pan, melt the chocolate chips, while continually stirring. Once smooth, begin dipping the balls into the chocolate mixture using a cocktail stick.

7. Place the balls to the baking sheet again and top with a pecan. This will cover any holes made by the cocktail stick.

8. Return the balls to the fridge until set.

9. Serve.

Mint Julep Fro-Yo

A classic cocktail classic comes to life as a frozen yogurt dessert. Serve at your next dinner party, and you are sure to make a good impression.

Servings: 4

Total Time: 3hour 15mins

Ingredients:

- ¾ cup bourbon (divided)
- ½ cup freshly packed mint leaves
- 1 cup sugar
- 3 cups low-fat yogurt
- ½ tsp peppermint essence

Directions:

1. In a pan, over moderate heat, combine ½ cup of the bourbon with the mint leaves and sugar. Take to a boil before turning the heat down and stewing until the sugar is entirely dissolved, and mint-infused in the bourbon, for approximately 10 minutes.

2. In a mixing bowl, combine the bourbon-sugar mixture with the yogurt, and peppermint essence. Chill in the fridge until totally cold, for 2 hours.

3. In you, ice cream maker, process the yogurt according to the manufacturer's directions, add in the remaining bourbon a little bit before the process is finished. Alternatively, and for an icier fro-yo freeze the mixture in a bowl and stir every 10-15 minutes until entirely.

Rice Pudding with Bourbon-Soaked Raisins

This recipe is perfect because the boozy dried fruit doesn't get added until the very end, meaning that everyone in your lovely family can enjoy the creamy rice pudding regardless of their age.

Servings: 6-8

Total Time: 1hour 15mins

Ingredients:

- ¾ cup raisins
- 3 tbsp bourbon
- 2 cups water
- 1 cup medium-grain white rice
- ¼ tsp salt
- 2½ cups whole milk
- 2½ cups half & half
- ⅔ cup granulated sugar
- 1½ tsp vanilla essence
- 1 tsp ground cinnamon

Directions:

1. In a tiny pan, combine the raisins with the bourbon and over moderate heat bring to simmer.

2. Once the mixture is simmering, remove the pan from the heat, cover with a lid, and put it to one side.

3. In a heavy pot of 3-4 quart capacity, bring 2 cups of water to boil. Stir in the rice along with the salt. Cover with a fitting lid and over low heat, simmer while stirring a couple of times until the water is almost entirely absorbed. This will take 15-20 minutes.

4. Pour in the milk and add the half & half along with the sugar.

5. Turn the heat up to moderate-high and bring it to simmer. Reduce heat to maintain at a simmer without allowing the mixture to come to a boil.

6. Cook, while frequently stirring and uncovered for half an hour, or until the mixture begins to thicken.

7. Reduce the heat down to low and continue cooking, stirring every 2-3 minutes to prevent sticking and scorching. The pudding is ready when a spoon is just capable of standing up in the rice pudding, for approximately an additional 15 minutes.

8. Take the pot out of the heat and stir in the boozy raisins, vanilla essence, and cinnamon.

9. Optional: Add an additional drop of bourbon, to taste.

10. Serve the pudding warm or chilled.

Sea Salt Bourbon Pecan Cookies

These nutty cookies with a bourbon glaze pair perfectly with coffee or hot chocolate and taste way better than any you can find in a shop.

Servings: 24

Total Time: 40mins

Ingredients:

Filling:

- 1 cup pecans (chopped)
- ½ cup brown sugar
- ¼ cup heavy cream
- Sea salt
- 1 tsp vanilla essence

Cookies:

- ¾ cup butter (softened)
- 1 cup brown sugar
- 1 egg
- 1 tsp vanilla essence
- 1 tsp baking powder
- 2 cups flour
- Salt

Glaze:

- 1 cup powdered sugar
- 2 tbsp bourbon
- 1 tbsp heavy cream

Directions:

1. Warm your main oven to 350 degrees F. Using parchment paper line 2 baking sheets. Put to one side.

2. In a bowl, add the filling Ingredients: pecans, brown sugar, heavy cream and a pinch of sea salt, to taste. Add the vanilla. Stir to incorporate and put to one side.

3. In a second, larger size bowl, for the cookies, cream the butter with the sugar, using a hand mixer.

4. Add the egg and vanilla essence, mixing to combine.

5. In a third smaller-size bowl, combine the baking powder with the flour, and pinch of salt, and whisk to combine.

6. Add half of the baking powder mixture to the butter mixture, and on the low-speed mix until the flour is entirely combined.

7. Add the remaining flour and mix until it has been added.

8. Using clean hands, shape the dough into 24 (1¼") balls.

9. Using vegetable spray, spray the back of a rounded teaspoon.

10. Make an indentation in the dough.

11. Add 1 teaspoon of the pecan filling to the indents.

12. Scatter a pinch of sea salt over the cookies and bake in the preheated oven for 8-12 minutes.

13. Transfer the cookies to the cooling wire baking rack.

14. For the glaze: In a bowl, combine the powdered sugar with the bourbon and heavy cream and stir until creamy smooth.

15. Drizzle the bourbon glaze over the cookies and set aside while the glaze sets and hardens.

16. Serve and enjoy.

Boozy Beverages

Bourbon Butterbeer

You can be sure that a grown-up Harry Potter would give this bourbon cocktail his seal of approval.

Servings: 1

Total Time: 4mins

Ingredients:

Syrup:

- ½ cup water
- ½ cup light brown sugar
- 1 tsp butter extract

Cocktail:

- 4 ounces apple cider
- 2 ounces ginger beer
- 1 ounce buttered brown sugar simple syrup
- 1½ ounces bourbon
- A pea-size chunk of dry ice*

Directions:

1. For the syrup: In a small pan, combine the water with the brown sugar and bring to boil. When sufficiently cooked, stir in the butter extract. Use as directed.

2. For the cocktail, combine the apple cider with the ginger beer, buttered brown sugar simple syrup, and bourbon.

3. Pour the drink into a glass mug.

4. Add the small piece of dry ice to the drink, allow to melt, and when the bubbling stops, enjoy.

Cook's Note: It is essential not to allow the dry ice to touch your skin or mouth. DO NOT DRINK DRY ICE.

Bourbon Cider

Enjoy the perfect fall cocktail as bourbon, and apple cider come together to create a sparkling drink.

Servings: 1

Total Time: 1hour 30mins

Ingredients:

Spiced Syrup:

- 1 cup sugar
- 1 (3") piece fresh ginger (peeled, finely sliced)
- 2 tbsp whole cloves (crushed)
- 1 cinnamon stick

Cocktail:

- 1½ ounces bourbon
- 3 ounces apple cider
- 1 tsp freshly squeezed lemon juice
- Slice of apple (to garnish)

Directions:

1. For the syrup: In a small pan, boil the water. Remove the pan from the heat and stir in the sugar followed by the ginger, cloves, and cinnamon stick. Set aside for 60 minutes. Strain and chill. This recipe makes approximately 1½ cups.

2. For the cocktail: In an ice-filled shaker, combine ¾ ounce of spiced syrup with the bourbon, apple cider, and lemon juice. Shake it all about.

3. Strain the cocktail into a martini glass.

4. Garnish with an apple slice and enjoy it.

Bourbon Eggnog

Festive Eggnog is a favorite yuletide beverage. This year, why not jazz it up with bourbon?

Servings: 12

Total Time:

Ingredients:

- 12 large-size egg yolks
- 2 cups sugar
- 4 cups cold milk
- 1 cup heavy cream
- 1½ cups bourbon
- 1 tsp vanilla essence
- Freshly grated nutmeg (to garnish)

Directions:

1. In your mixing bowl, whisk the egg yolks with the sugar until frothy and smooth.

2. Whisk in the milk followed by the cream, bourbon, and vanilla essence.

3. Transfer to a punch bowl or pitcher.

4. Sprinkle with freshly grated nutmeg and serve.

Bubbles 'n Bourbon Cocktail

The best of both worlds as chilled, fizzy Champagne combines with smoky bourbon to create a sophisticated cocktail for one.

Servings: 1

Total Time: 5mins

Ingredients:

- Ice
- 2 ounces bourbon
- ½ ounce freshly squeezed lemon juice
- ¾ ounce simple syrup
- 3 dashes of Angostura bitters
- Champagne (chilled, as needed)

Directions:

1. Add the ice to a highball glass.

2. Pour over the bourbon, fresh lemon juice, syrup, and bitters.

3. Gently stir and fill with Champagne.

4. Enjoy.

Burnt Orange Bourbon

Burnt orange brings a rich, smoky sweetness to this elegant cocktail.

Servings: 1

Total Time:

Ingredients:

- ½ orange (seeded, cut into 4 slices)
- 1 tbsp sugar
- 1 cup ice
- Freshly squeezed juice of ½ orange
- 2 ounce bourbon
- Slices of burnt orange (to serve)

Directions:

1. Heat your oven on grill.

2. Place the slices of orange on a greased baking sheet.

3. Sprinkle the sugar over the oranges.

4. Grill the orange until lightly browned and a little burnt.

5. Take the baking sheet out of the oven and allow the oranges to cool.

6. Fill a large-size glass with ice followed by 2 slices of orange, orange juice, and bourbon.

7. Muddle the cocktail and strain into a large serving glass.

8. Garnish with the remaining slices of burnt orange and enjoy.

Caramel Bourbon Milkshake

Shakes things up a little and add bourbon to a creamy milkshake. Serve with a tall spoon and straw.

Servings: 1

Total Time: 6mins

Ingredients:

- 2 cups vanilla ice cream
- 2 ounces caramel sauce
- 1 ounce heavy whipping cream
- 1½ ounces bourbon
- Pinch of salt
- Whipped cream (to serve, optional)
- Caramel sauce (store-bought, to garnish)

Directions:

1. In the freezer, chill a tall glass.

2. In a blender, combine the ice cream with the caramel sauce, heavy whipping cream, bourbon and a pinch of salt. Process until combined.

3. Pour the milkshake into the tall, chilled glass.

4. Top with a dollop of whipped cream and a drizzle of caramel sauce.

5. Serve with a tall spoon and straw and enjoy.

Grapefruit Bourbon Yule Mule

Sharp grapefruit juice, spicy ginger beer, and smoky bourbon are the ultimate cocktail combination. Serve with a sprig of fragrant rosemary.

Servings: 1

Total Time: 4mins

Ingredients:

- 3 ounces freshly squeezed grapefruit juice
- 1¾ ounce mini bottle bourbon
- 3 ounces ginger beer
- Ice (to serve)
- A sprig of rosemary (to garnish)

Directions:

1. Pour the grapefruit juice along with the bourbon into a nickel-lined copper cup.

2. Top with ginger beer.

3. Add a couple of ice cubes and garnish with a sprig of rosemary.

4. Enjoy.

Kentucky Coffee

Feeling the cold? Then this bourbon-spiked coffee will soon warm you up!

Servings: 4

Total Time: 10mins

Ingredients:

- 8 cubes of sugar
- 12 tbsp premium bourbon
- 4 cups freshly brewed, strong coffee (hot)
- ½ cup heavy cream (lightly whipped)

Directions:

1. Put 2 cubes of sugar into 4 (12 ounce) coffee mugs.

2. Add 3 tablespoons of bourbon to each of the 4 coffee mugs. With a muddler, muddle the sugar together with the bourbon until the sugar entirely dissolves.

3. Pour 1 cup of strong hot coffee into each of the mugs.

4. Rest the back of a teaspoon against the inside of the mug. Slowly pour the whipped cream into the mug.

5. Serve and enjoy.

Kentucky Iced Tea

Afternoon tea has a completely new meaning with this boozy beverage featuring not one but four alcoholic ingredients.

Servings: 12-14

Total Time: 6mins

Ingredients:

- ½ ounce bourbon
- ½ ounce gin
- ½ ounce vodka
- ½ ounce triple sec
- ½ ounce freshly squeezed lemon juice
- Ice
- Lemon and lime soda (chilled)
- Lemon wedges (to serve)

Directions:

1. In a cocktail shaker, combine the bourbon, gin, vodka, triple sec, and fresh lemon juice, ice. Shake it all about.

2. Strain the tea into a chilled and ice-filled Tom Collins glass.

3. Add sufficient lemon and lime soda, to fill the glass, stir gently and serve with a wedge of lemon.

Voodoo Daiquiri

Go to the dark side with this devilish daiquiri.

Servings: 2

Total Time: 3mins

Ingredients:

- 4 ounces bourbon
- 2 ounces vodka
- 8 ounces grape juice
- 2 cups crushed ice

Directions:

1. Add the bourbon, vodka and grape juice to a blender. On moderate speed, blend until smooth, for 60 seconds.

2. Pour the cocktail into 2 crushed-ice filled glasses.

3. Serve and enjoy.

Author's Afterthoughts

thank you

I would like to express my deepest thanks to you, the reader, for making this investment in one my books. I cherish the thought of bringing the love of cooking into your home.

With so much choice out there, I am grateful you decided to Purch this book and read it from beginning to end.

Please let me know by submitting an Amazon review if you enjoyed this book and found it contained valuable information to help you in your culinary endeavors. Please take a few minutes to express your opinion freely and honestly. This will help others make an informed decision on purchasing and provide me with valuable feedback.

Thank you for taking the time to review!

Christina Tosch

About the Author

Christina Tosch is a successful chef and renowned cookbook author from Long Grove, Illinois. She majored in Liberal Arts at Trinity International University and decided to pursue her passion of cooking when she applied to the world renowned Le Cordon Bleu culinary school in Paris, France. The school was lucky to recognize the immense talent of this chef and she excelled in her courses, particularly Haute Cuisine. This skill was recognized and rewarded by several highly regarded Chicago restaurants, where she was offered the prestigious position of head chef.

Christina and her family live in a spacious home in the Chicago area and she loves to grow her own vegetables and herbs in the garden she lovingly cultivates on her sprawling estate. Her and her husband have two beautiful children, 3 cats, 2 dogs and a parakeet they call Jasper. When Christina is not hard at work creating beautiful meals for Chicago's elite, she is hard at work writing engaging e-books of which she has sold over 1500.

Make sure to keep an eye out for her latest books that offer helpful tips, clear instructions and witty anecdotes that will bring a smile to your face as you read!

CPSIA information can be obtained
at www.ICGtesting.com
Printed in the USA
BVHW030817220421
605628BV00008B/29